Yo Capeesh!

Yo Capeesh!

✦

A Guide to Understanding Italian Americans

Jim Caridi

Writers Club Press
New York Lincoln Shanghai

Yo Capeesh!
A Guide to Understanding Italian Americans

Writers Club Press
an imprint of iUniverse, Inc.

For information address:
iUniverse
2021 Pine Lake Road, Suite 100
Lincoln, NE 68512
www.iuniverse.com

Not for the politically correct

ISBN: 0-595-22168-8

Printed in the United States of America

To ma famiglia, biologic and chosen.

Acknowledgement

A heartfelt grazie to my brother Robert, my wife Rhonda, my Mom and my most loyal friend Rich (rainy face) Stanton. Their enthusiasm, support and inspiration provided me with the courage to cross that formidable bridge that starts with an idea and ends with reality. They reminded me that the experience of crossing that bridge was worth more than any reward that could be found on the other side. They were right. We reminisced, we learned, we laughed, we cried. I got to go home again. What more could I ask? Salute!!!

Contents

Introduction

As an author of several scientific articles and related book chapters it was not customary for me to venture outside my field. I embarked upon this project in response to a fascination of my children with the "old ways".

Because my education led me to settle in a fairly homogeneous Southern town, many of my traditions, mannerisms and lingo were not familiar to our friends and neighbors. This didn't bother me but apparently it was somewhat disturbing to my children. Recently, however, the media has reversed this feeling by injecting the public with this fascination for the Italian American way of life, stereotypical or not. Now my kids are like sponges trying to soak up all the old stories, names and traditions. I guess now it is "cool" to be Italian. Therefore, to help my children, I thought I'd write a little guide to familiarize them with those foods, phrases, mannerisms and expressions used by the media to make us cool.

What I found was my own epiphany. The many memories, traditions and uniquenesses that I had as a child had been diluted by assimilation and technology. As I researched some of the lists in this book, I contacted old relatives, relived old stories and spent time around those people and things that were Italian American. I use this distinction frequently in the book. Italian Americans are a subculture of their Italian brethren. The demands of immigration and assimilation led to a massaging of many of the traditions and language. It also led to a unique group of productive and talented citizens. You know, I forgot how cool it was to be Italian American. Actually, I forgot how cool it is.

This guide was written primarily for entertainment. It is intended to be both amusing and at times educational. It was never intended to be disrespectful. I ardently believe that laughter is essential to the physical and mental well being of an individual. I also believe that anyone with the ability to laugh at him or herself will be guaranteed a limitless supply of humor. Good health to you all.

Words to play bocce by

   The following is by no means an Italian dictionary, nor is it meant to be. In fact some words are not even Italian but represent a hybridization of Italian and immigrant dialect. Until recently, I thought that "bah-cows" was Italian for bathroom. My daughter, who studies formal Italian, informed me that I was far from correct. When I investigated the origin of "bah-cows", I found that it was what the early immigrants referred to as the outhouse. That was, the back-a-house.

For those who enjoy Italian American movies and TV, the words listed below can serve as a guide. Just one or two of these words are often interjected into a sentence for emphasis or to create that Italian mystique. As most people know, Italian Americans have the uncanny ability to send a message, or make a point just by uttering one or two words combined with some animated gesture. Many of the words have a loose or regional interpretation but their implication is usually obvious. To assist in their search and correct pronunciation, the words are spelled phonetically. Although these words should be helpful for interpreting the obscure clichés found in movies and TV, I have also found them useful at feasts, restaurants and, of course, a good game of bocce.

Ah-coo-cah—	go to sleep
Ahn-dee-am-o—	let's go
Ahh-jih-da—	heartburn, chest pain, used like "Terry, your mother gives me "ahh-jih-da"
Ahh-riv-a-der-chi—	good bye, rarely used
A-more-ay—	love
Baah-cows—	bathroom derived from "back house" when outhouses were in vogue
Baad-a-boom—	commonly said with a gesture (jab), used to make a point or exclamation; often followed by baad-a-bing
Bah-n-yo—	bathroom, formal
Bah-sta—	enough, usually said repetitively like basta, basta, basta
Bam-bee-noh—	baby
Bear-troom—	another pronunciation of bathroom, common Brooklynese
Beh-doik-yas—	bugs, used like—hey, you got beh-doik-yas, usually said when someone is scratching a lot. (a common trait among Italian American males)
Bell-ah-ma-ma—	beautiful, pretty, commonly expressed by Moms

Ben-ven-u-to—	welcome, the key word for defining a chain food restaurant as "Italian"
Bew-tee-ful—	beautiful, with emphasis on the tee
Bone-a-pih-teet—	good appetite
Boo-la-shin-gool—	ants in the pants, fidgety, "Yo, Vito, sit! You got a boo-la-shin-gool ????"
Bos-oh-why—	someone who is a piss and moan, complainer
Bru-to—	ugly
Bun-jor-no—	hello, good day
Bwo-nah-sara—	good evening
Cah-sa—	house
Cah-la-braze—	from Calabria, slang for thickheaded. What are you cah-la-braze?
Ca-peesh—	understand, commonly used alone after a statement to ensure that the other party understood the message. Ca-peesh?
Chin-don—	for a hundred years, frequently used as a toast
Chow (ciao)—	hello, good-bye,
Co-meh-sta—	how are you? a common greeting
Cosi—cosi—	so so
Cuu-chee-na—	kitchen, the heart of the Italian American home
Don't bust my chops—	don't annoy me, knock it off
Earl—	Brooklynese for oil, also used by some from New Orleans
Eay—	hey, what, yeah or an exclamation
Ehn-gup-a-nor-na—	swear on your grandmother's grave
Fah-jay-brute—	ugly face
Fes-ta—	Feast
Fug-ged—abou-dit—	don't worry about it, no problem, drop it, or just forget about it
Fu-gay-zee—	fake

Ga-goots—	really a squash, slang for squat, nothing—used as "I ain't got ga-goots"
Get the "F" outta Heeh—	you must be kidding!
Giz-u-chase—	what happened?
Giz-ah-deesh—	what have you got to say, essentially an informal greeting
Good as bread—	if you're good as bread, you're the best because nothing beats Italian bread
Goom-bah or (goom-bah-da)—	close friend, best man, godfather
Gotz-ahs—	junk, trinkets
Grat-zee—	thank you
Heeh—	here
I-yuu-da—	help!!, usually followed by Jazz-u-greest
Jazz-u-greest—	Jesus Christ, usually used with I-yuu-da Jazz-u-greest
Jeet—	did you eat? commonly followed by no jew (no did you)
Jesus, Mary & Joseph—	an emphatic expression for anytime someone is upset, mad or surprised (often a cue for you to run, hide or shut up)
Kay-cose-et-chose—	how's things, informal greeting
La fam-eel-ya—	The family, the sacred heart of Italian culture
Maah—	Mother, the unofficial head of the Italian family, the heart of the Italian male, his Achilles heel, commonly expressed as a whine
Maah-done—	Madonna (the original) usually used to express surprise, wow, holy smoke!
Mah-naa-jia—	damn
Mal-oik-ya—	the feared evil eye that Italians deliver or attempt to avoid by wearing the Italian horn
Med-ee-gone—	non-Italians, i.e. Americans
Men-za men-za—	so-so; half, half

Meh-ta-bah-uud—	afraid
Momma-mee-a—	an exclamation e.g. holy mackerel! enough! Literally, my mother
Mezz-a-mort—	half dead, the way you feel after a night drinking grappa
Miz-a-daab-la—	miserable person
More-ta—	dead
N-grat-zee-a-da—	ungrateful
Nob-al-dee-don—	from Naples
Nuum-ash-port-ta-da bust-a-chor-ta-da—	don't bust my chops
Ooo-fah—	expression meaning that's tough or forget about it
Ott—so—	gee whiz, that's enough
Pal (paly)—	generic word for someone, like hey pal, yo pal, forget about it pal.
Pots—	crazy, are you pots? When disagreeing just utter an emphatic, Pots!
Pie-san—	friend, can be used to define members of a group. His paisans.
Pis-sah—	something that is funny, that's a pis-sah (pisser)
Pear-fa-vor-ay—	please
Prey-go—	not the sauce but just about anything else—good, thanks, you're welcome
Puut-za—	smells
Rosa , I'm home—	Italian foreplay
Sa-luut—	"to your health" said while having a drink , toasting, usually with glasses held high
Sang-which—	sandwich
Scutch—	someone who is very annoying or an act of annoyance
Scuu-zee	excuse me
Seh-ta—	sit
Shpit-a-bock—	messy

Shh-skieve—	be afraid of, something that disgusts you, or turns your stomach
Shum-in-eed—	dopey, stupid
Siz-iliee-yano—	from Sicily
S'matter—	what's the matter?
Son-a-ma-gun—	son of a gun, nice way to say son a ma b*tch
Stah-ta-born—	be well, common expression used instead of good bye
Stahn-ga—	tired
Stah-ta-seet—	be quiet, shaddup!
Sto-bee-n—	I am well
Sto-mahl—	I am bad
Su-jeh-ta—	obligated, indebted
The old country—	Italy
Turl-ette—	Brooklynese for toilet
Whats a matter you—	what is the matter?
Yo—	hey

Body language—let-a you hands do the talking

Italian Americans are among the most expressive and animated people on the planet. They are maestros of non-verbal communication. It is as if they are conducting their thoughts as they speak. A picture may be worth a thousand words, but a hand gesture can send an entire message. Some of which are not so nice-a. One thing is for certain; you don't have to worry about misinterpretation or being misquoted.

Hand and body gesturing may have originated out of necessity. Since the volume of a typical Italian American discussion, pleasant or not, exceeds the obnoxious level for most individuals, body language ensures that the intended message is conveyed. Probably more important than this is the fact that manual expression allows for the simultaneous enjoyment of two of their favorite pastimes: eating and talking.

However, one must be wary of the perpetrator of conversational violence. This is the guy who subconsciously delivers non-fatal jabs throughout an entire conversation. He uses them like physical exclamation points. Following a family gathering, the number of bruises on my thigh and arm were visual reminders of the conversations with Uncle Sonny.

In general, the gesticulations of Italian Americans are choreographic expressions of emotion and feeling. Many times these are even amusing. You might say Italian Americans have always had ESP, that is, Extremities Say Plenty.

I-yuu-da—help me. What do they want from me Lord? If the hands are moved back and forth in the praying position either pointed up or down it can represent a big question mark. What are they doing? How could they do this?

An expression of good quality. Bellisimo. That's-a so nice. That tastes good. She looks great.

This is a half bah-fon-gool (go "F" yourself). Either the intended recipient didn't do something that bad or the sender is lazy. The right hand, palm down, is slapped over the elbow portion of the left arm as it is swung straight up.

The Italian salute. This is the full bah-fon-gool. There is no mistaking this one. It means business. The palm of the right hand is slapped in the flexed elbow portion of the left arm. To add an exclamation point the hand can be twisted down at the end of the movement. Best performed with an audible "God Bless You"!!!

Fon-ob-ah-la. Go to Naples. Go to hell. I couldn't care less!! The last 4 fingers are in a semi-fist position and dragged under the chin, making sure to scratch the chin just before they are thrust forward. The movement finishes by pointing the fingers straight up.

Hold me back. You really give me ahh-jih-da. You piss me off. The knuckle of the second finger is placed between the teeth and bitten while the hand is in a fist.

Basically, how the "F" do I know? Or, I don't know nothin. The shoulders are hunched and the hands are open signifying a big question mark.

I'm axing a question here. What do you want from me? Notice the difference from the previous picture. Here the shoulders are down and the fingers are together.

How, what, when, where, what do you mean, how did that happen?
Basically any question. With arm bent, just turn the right hand up bring the
fingers together and wave the hand back and forth. No words are necessary.

Mah-naa-jia (damn) you piss me off. First bite that unnamed skin between your thumb and forefinger. Then turn your hand up, bring your fingers together and wave them back and forth. This can also be performed without the second hand.

Giving the mal-oik-ya. Casting the evil eye. The ring and middle fingers are folded in as the pinky and forefinger are straight forward. The whole hand is jabbed forward in this position toward the intended object. This also can be used with the half bah-fon-gool.

Usually performed with an audible—Heeh!!!! (here). A simple gesture to indicate that you don't necessarily agree. It can also mean you want a piece of me?

A synonym for the previous gesture. It also is an exclamation of disagreement. It can be performed with an audible—you can put that right heeh. (self-explanatory)

Oh maa-done! Kay puut-za (what smells)? Get it out-ta heeh. Just hold the nose with one hand and wave the other.

I'm thinking.

I need a manicure.

Italian American Heroes

Vincent Caridi and Esther Ardolino 1921

Italians and later Italian Americans have played an integral role in the success and development of the United States as a nation. It began with the likes of Christopher Columbus, John Cabot (Giovanni Caboto),

Giovanni Verazanno and Amerigo Vespucci—all of whom were responsible for exploring the western hemisphere and opening it to the migration of Europeans. Despite the wave of recent political correctness, their bravery and impact cannot be denied. Just ask my Uncle Vito who never misses a Columbus Day parade. From the days of exploration to present day, the Italian American influence has permeated all aspects of American culture. True, the majority of Italians came to America from 1890 to 1920, but noted Italian Americans also fought in the Revolutionary and Civil Wars.

To truly understand Italian Americans one must be acquainted with the individuals they worship. This includes their heroes and their icons. For Italian Americans, the most idolized individuals are either reproduced as a statue and/or are commemorated as a parade, feast or pastry. The following list of "heroes" is by no means complete, however, it does underscore the positive, pervasive impact of a culture that politicians and journalists early in the 1900's referred to as "mongrels", "dregs", "kidnappers", "murderers", "lazy", "asocial" and "worthless".

Christopher Columbus: The man who made it all happen. Despite all the current controversy, you would be hard pressed to convince most real Italian Americans that he is not worthy of the claim that he discovered America. In most Italian communities he is still honored annually with a parade on October 12.

Madonna: The virgin, not the singer. The Virgin Mary holds a special place in the hearts and worship of Italian Americans. She is idolized with jewelry and statues. It is common to see her statue displayed in the yard under a small enclosure sometimes referred to as "Mary in the shell". When Italian Americans first moved from the city to suburbia, Mary in the shell came before curtains or furniture.

St. Anthony: Patron saint of lost items. If you can't find something he's the guy you want. Pray to him (especially on Tuesday night) and you'll find it. He apparently knows where everything is. His feast day is June 13.

St. Joseph: The patron saint of family life. A statue of him is often seen standing on his head. Reportedly, if you want to sell your house you are supposed to turn him upside down and place him in your backyard. He is so well liked he also rates a pastry. Also, the Feast (la Festa) of San Giuseppe is commemorated yearly in many Italian American homes on March 19.

St. Theresa: Patron Saint of France. Known as the Little Flower and the Little Flower of Jesus. Someone to pray to when you have problems or need help. Her feast day is October 1.

St. Rocco: Patron Saint of Patrica Italy. Also, the protector against plague and contagious disease. He is celebrated by a feast in July.

San Gennaro: Patron Saint of Naples. Commemorated in September by the largest feast in Little Italy, New York. La Festa di tutti la Festa!!

Artists:

Constantino Brumidi—	painted the ceiling of the US capital dome as well as many Capitol frescos
Charles Nolcini—	Composer, organist and teacher in the 1800's
Andrea Palotti—	designed Monticello (little mountain) for Thomas Jefferson
Attilio Piccirilli—	carved the statue of Lincoln for the Lincoln Memorial
Frank Stella—	abstract painter

Authors:

Hamilton Basso	John Ciardi
Don Delillo	Bernard De Voto Lawrence Feringhetti
Jerre Mangione	Mario Puzo
Gay Telese	Franco Zeffirelli

Educators

Frances Xavier Cabrini—	responsible for establishing Colombia Hospital, she was also the first American Saint
John Cataldo—	founded Gonzaga University
Renato Dulbecco—	one of three who won the Nobel Prize in genetics— 1975
Enrico Fermi—	awarded the Nobel Prize for Physics in 1938
Robert Gallo—	co-discovered the AIDS virus as well as a test for it
Giovanni Battista Grassi—	received the Darwin Medal for his work with malaria
John Grassi—	first president of Georgetown University
Louis Ignarro—	won the Nobel Prize in Medicine in 1998
Gaetano Lanza—	founded the engineering department at MIT
Salvador Luria—	won the Nobel Prize in 1969 for Physiology/Medicine
Marconi—	awarded the Nobel Prize for work in wireless technology
Filippo Mazzei—	his philosophy influenced Thomas Jefferson in the wording of the Declaration of Independence
Franco Modigliani—	won the Nobel Prize in Economics in 1985
Rita Levi-Montalcini—	won the Nobel Prize in Medicine in 1986
Dr. Maria Montessori—	her philosophies influenced private education in the U.S.
Sylvia Scaramelli—	co-founded Fairleigh Dickenson University
Emilio Segre—	won the Nobel Prize for Physics in 1959

Entrepreneurs:

Joseph Barbera—	co-owner of Hanna-Barbera cartoon studio
Michael Bongiovanni—	retired president and CEO of Squibb Corporation
Dan and Frank Carney—	opened the first Pizza Hut
Bernard Castro—	invented the Castro convertible sofa
Vincent R. Ciccone—	invented the cough drop and blow pop
Anthony Conza—	established the first Blimpie sandwich shop
Nicholas D'Agostino—	developed the first supermarket concept combining meat, groceries and a bakery in one store (D'Agastino Chain)
Edward J. DeBartolo—	began first shopping plazas / malls
Fred DeLuca—	founded the Subway sandwich chain
Ernest & Julio Gallo—	founded the E & J Gallo winery
Domenico Ghirardelli—	developed a technique to produce ground chocolate
A.P. Giannini—	with 5 partners started the Bank of Italy which became the Bank of America
Felix Grucci Sr—	started a world renowned fireworks company
Lee Iacocca—	saved the Chrysler Corporation from bankruptcy
Roy Jacuzzi—	invented the Jacuzzi
Italo Marcioni—	invented the ice cream cone
Guglelmo Marconi—	perfected the wireless telegraph and invented the radio
Antonio Meucci—	the true inventor of the telephone
Amedeo Obici / Mario Peruzzi—	started the Planter's peanut company
Jeno Paulucci—	created Chun King, first chairman of RJ Reynolds Foods
Leonardo Riggio—	founder of Barnes and Noble bookstores
Anthony Rossi—	founded the Tropicana fruit company

Entertainers:

Danny Aiello
Alan Alda (Alphonso D'Abruzzo)
Don Ameche
Armand Assante
Frankie Avalon
Scott Baio
Ann Bancroft (Italiano)
Tony Bennett
Valerie Bertonelli
Robert Blake
John Bon Jovi
Sonny Bono
Ernest Borgnine
Marlon Brando
Steve Buscemi
Ruth Buzzi
Nicholas Cage (Coppola)
Frank Capra
Carmine Caridi
Madonna Ciccone
Imogene Coca
Pat Cooper (Pasquale Caputo)
Lou Costello
Enrico Caruso
Perry Como
Francis Ford Coppola
Vic Damone
Tony Danza
Bobby Darin (Cassotto)
James Darren (Ercolani)

Sandra Dee

Dom DeLuise

Robert Deniro

Brian De Palma

Danny DeVito

Leonardo DiCaprio

Jimmy Durante

James Farentino

Lou Ferrigno

Connie Francis (Concetta Franconero)

Annette Funicello

Janeane Garofalo

Ben Gazzara

Rita Hayworth (Margarita Cansino)

Billy Joel

Nick La Rocca

Mario Lanza

Jay Leno

Tea Leoni (Pantleoni)

Liberace

Ray Liotta

Guy Lombardo

Susan Lucci

Dan Luria

Penny Marshall (Masciarelli)

Dean Martin (Dino Paul Crocetti)

Henri Mancini

Liza Minelli

Sal Mineo

Lou Monte

Joe Montegna

Al Pacino

Chazz Palminteri

Joe Pesci

Bernadette Peters (Lazzara)

Regis Philbin

Joe Piscopo

Louis Prima

Christina Ricci

Ray Romano

Cesar Romero

Susan Sarandon (Tomaling)

Neil Sedaka

Connie Selleca

Frank Sinatra

Martin Scorcese

Paul Sorvino

John Philip Sousa

Bruce Springsteen

Sylvester Stallone

Connie Stevens

Quentin Tarantino

Marisa Tomei

Arturo Toscanini

John Travolta

Steven Tyler (Tallarico)

Brenda Vaccaro

Steven Vai

Rudolf Valentino

Jerry Vale

Frankie Valli (Castellucio)

Pia Zadora (Schipani)

Frank Zappa

Politicians:

Sonny Bono—	Congressman
Joseph Califano—	Secretary of Health Education and Welfare
Richard Celeste—	Governor
Argeo Cellucci—	Governor
Mario Cuomo—	Governor
Alfonse D'Amato—	Senator
Christopher Del Sesto—	Governor
Edward DiPrete—	Governor
Michael Di Salle—	Governor
Peter Domenici—	Senator
Geraldine Ferraro—	first woman to run for Vice President
James Florio—	Governor
Foster Furcolo—	Governor
Rudolph Giuliani—	Mayor
Ella Grasso—	Governor
Fiorello LaGuardia—	Mayor
Rick Lazio—	Congressman
Andrew Longino—	Governor
John Marchi—	Senator
Susan Molinari—	Congresswoman
John Notte—	Governor
William Paca—	first Italian American Governor (Maryland 1782)
John Pastore—	first Italian American elected to the U.S. senate (1950-79)
George Pataki—	Governor
John Phinizy—	first Italian American Mayor (Augusta, GA 1837)
Charles Poletti—	Governor
Peter Rodino—	U.S. Congressman
Onario Razzolino—	First Italian to hold office in U.S.
Frank Rizzo	Commissioner, Mayor

Alberto D. Rosselini—	Governor
Angelo J. Rossi—	Mayor
Alfred E. Smith—	(born Alfred Emanuele Ferraraand) first Italian American Governor of New York, also ran for president against Herbert Hoover
Anthony Scalia—	Supreme Court Justice
John Sirica—	Watergate Judge
Angelo Siringo—	Lawman who captured Billy the Kid
Francis B. Spinola—	first U.S. Italian American Congressman (1887)
Robert Torricelli—	Senator
John Volpe—	Governor

Sports figures:

Atlas (Angelo Siciliana)

Mario Andretti

Eddie Arcaro

Sal Bando

Yogi Berra

Brian Boitano

Nick Buoniconti

Roy Campanella

Jennifer Capriati

Angelo Dundee

Joe DiMaggio

Carl Furillo

Joe Garagiola

A. Bartlett Giamatti

Rocky Graziano

Franco Harris

Jake LaMotta

Tommy Lasorda

Tony Lazzeri
Vincent Lombardi
Ed Marinaro
Billy Martin (Alfred Pesano)
Rocky Marziano
Joe Montana
Willie Mosconi
Joe Paterno
Joe Pepitone
Mike Piazza
Lou Pinella
Rick Pitino
Mary Lou Retton
Phil Rizzuto
Vinny Testaverde
Joe Torre
Frank Viola

Finally, a salute to some real heroes, the 1.5 million Italian Americans who fought in the U.S. armed forces in World War II. They made up the largest percentage of any ethnic group fighting for the U.S.. Reportedly they comprised 20% of all U.S. forces. Quite remarkable, considering some were fighting against their family members or their parents' country of origin.

Names and (Nicknames)

An individual's name or nickname has always been a vital part of the Italian American persona. Most commonly, the names originate out of honor or respect for one or more family members. Titles are taken very seriously. The first, middle and confirmation names should flow like Chianti. Naming someone after a celebrity is just not an option. The following section includes a list of names followed by nicknames that have been used to underscore Italian American heritage.

Names for your bambinos

Priests (boys)

Alfonso	Angelo	Anthony
Antonio	Augie	Bruno
Carlo	Carmine	Dante
Dominick	Enrico	Enzo
Francesco	Franco	Gaspare
Geno	Giacomo	Giorgio
Giovanni	Giuesspe	Junior
Lanzo	Leo	Luigi
Marco	Mario	Muno
Nino	Nunzio	Pauli
Primo	Rocco	Rocky
Salvatore	Sylvio	Tony
Vincenzo	Vinny	Vito

Nuns (girls)

Adelaide	Adriana	Anastasia
Andrea	Angelina	Annamarria
Anunziata	Carlota	Carmela
Caterina	Christina	Cristiana
Daniela	Felicia	Filomena
Francesca	Gabriella	Geena
Giovina	Gisella	Juliana
Leena	Lisa	Margarita
Mariana	Mary	Nina
Pia	Raffaella	Rosa
Rosalie	Rosemarie	Rosie
Stella	Suzetta	Teresa
Tessa	Tessie	Theresa

(((Nicknames)))

Although common throughout many cultures, Italian Americans are the masters of nicknames. Perhaps this arises from their genetic creativity. Having a nickname, however, can go either way. It may represent a status symbol or, on the other hand, can be somewhat demeaning. In either case, once it sticks, it is yours forever, no matter how old or what the occasion. If you are 85 years old, 280 pounds and dead, it doesn't matter, you are still "little Pauli".

Regarding nicknames, two things are for certain. You don't appoint yourself a nickname, and you hope you don't have one of which you are unaware. Basically if you have to give yourself a nickname it might as well be "the loser". Alternatively, the pinnacle of nicknamery is to see your moniker printed between your first and last names while enclosed in parentheses.

Nicknames arise from a multitude of sources. They can be clever aberrations of a person's name, occupation, physical appearance, personality, resemblance to some other living thing or because everyone in the family ended up with the same name. In my family it was Frankie and Joey. For people who were descendents of both the Roman Empire and the Renaissance, how imaginative was it to pick 5 Frankies and 7 Joeys. Well, in deference to my family, these names often arose out of respect for the paternal lineage (also all named Frankie and Joey). So, out of sheer necessity, sometimes referred to as creativity, came the nicknames, (big Frankie), (little Frankie), (cousin Frankie), (Frankie 3 fingers) and finally (Frankie the phlegm).

The following are some legendary nicknames that made it into (parentheses).

Animals:

Ape man, the bull, chicken man, morning doves, the animal, the hawk, the weasel, chicken head, the camel, jackass, the horse.

Physical Appearance:

Bony, blackie, the brain, legs, blue eyes, blue jaw, the boot, the chin, cockeyed, creepy, the devil, fat, handsome, greasy thumb, happy, humpy, lefty, legs, longy, mad dog, nails, pretty, no nose, the scourge, shorty, skinny, terrible, teets, tough, tutti.

Food and Professions:

Apples, bananas, beans, the boss, bottles, cookie, the doctor, figs, the gardener, golf bag, the gyp, the killer, the lackey, lucky, the plumber, pork chops, peppers, plums, the schemer, shotgun, socks, two gun.

Mangia, mangia, eat-a, eat-a

No one likes food, or for that matter does it better, than Italian Americans. The garden of colors and fragrances from the typical Italian spread is enough to exhaust any salivary gland. Food and the kitchen are the mainstay of the Italian American culture around which everything revolves. Gravy means it's Sunday. Zeppole is Christmas, pizza grano is Easter. To this day, I would swear that football games have a half time to avoid interrupting the Sunday afternoon dinner. Likewise, when entertaining family or friends, where did everyone congregate? In the kitchen. It was a necessity to have a long table and lots of extra chairs. Ott-so!! You could never buy a house with only a nook. Those houses were for the medigones.

Since many of us, Italian American or not, have different traditions, we may not always be familiar with the endless variety of Italian foods now readily available to everyone. Also, some of those economical concoctions that Ma whipped up in an instant are now under an assumed gourmet name in pricey Italian restaurants. What I called potatoes and eggs is now a frittata. This chapter is a simple reference for the common Italian foods found not only in some Italian restaurants but also in Ma's kitchen. Use it as a guide or to impress your paisans. For those of you who are familiar with all of the foods, hopefully it will nourish some good memories.

For those of you who need it, the words are also spelled phonetically. This was included because there is nothing that torques my linguine or gives me more ahh-jih-da than going to an "Italian" restaurant and hearing… mair-in-air-a or mozz-a-rella. Especially when it is the waiter.

Prior to eating, regardless of how much screaming and yelling or how good or bad the day, each dinner had to be started with grace. The classic Italian American grace (much of which went so fast it sounded like gibberish) usually sounded like: Bless us oh Lord for these Thy gifts we are about to receive from Thy bounty of Christ, oh Lord, Amen. That was the cue for someone (usually Ma) to say a hearty Bone-a-pih-teet!!!! Then from across the table, the finale, thank you Lord.

Al dente (al-den-tay)—	pasta cooked so that it is still firm
Alfredo (al-frey-doe)—	crème and cheese sauce
Antipasto (ahn-tee-pah-sta)—	appetizers, usually salami, peppers, olives, bread, cheese served before the main meal
Arrabbiata (ah-rah-bi-ah-ta)—	tomato sauce with mushrooms, hot peppers and basil
Asiago (ah-see-ah-go)—	a cow's milk cheese that is not as sharp as provolone

Baked goods:

Biscotti (bish-caught)—	long hard biscuit or cookie twice baked
Cannoli (con-oh-lee)—	sweetened ricotta cheese filled tubular pastry
Panforte (pan-for-tee)—	spiced fruit and nut cake
Pasticciotti (pass-tih-chi-ote-tee)—	vanilla or chocolate custard filled pastry
Pignoli (pin-yo-lee) cookies—	cookies made with pine nuts
Pizza grano (peat-sa-gran)—	grain pie served at Easter
Pizza rustica (peat-sa-rue-stee-ka)—	flaky pastry layered with meats, mozzerella and eggs
Sfingi (spheen-ga)—	a big puff pastry with ricotta cream filling (St. Josephs)
Sfogliatella (shh-vool-ya-del)—	clam shaped crusty pastry filled with ricotta cheese
Struffoli (stru-fa-lee)—	small fried dough balls served with honey and sprinkles
Tar-tu-fo (tar-tu-foe)—	Italian truffles
Tiramisu (tier-a-mee-su)—	lady fingers, whipped cream, marscopone cheese, gran marnier flavor, expresso (means "pick me up")
Tor-one (tore-own)—	nougat candy

Zeppole (zape-oh-la)—   fried dough balls served with powered sugar commonly made on Christmas morning and become dough rocks by Christmas night

Foods Continued

Baccala (bach-ah-la)—   a smelly fish, also slang for female anatomy

Baz-inee-gole—   basil, often grown in a "garden"—a small patch of herbs

Bolognese (bol-on-aise) sauce—   meat sauce often made with wine and tomatoes

Braciole (bra-shole)—   rolled meat, beef, tied with pastry string

Broccoli rabe (brook-a-lee-raab)—   greens that look like grass, taste like weeds, very bitter, eaten with Italian bread and lots of salt

Bruschetta (bru-sheh-ta)—   toasted bread topped with garlic and olive oil

Carbonara (caab-on-ara)—   sauce made of garlic, bacon and eggs

Cacciatore (catch-ah-tor-ee)—   vegetables cooked in a thick sauce with meat

Calamari (cal-a-maad)—   squid

Calzone (cal-zone)—   stuffed folded pizza

Cannellini (can-ah-leen-ee)—   white kidney beans

Cappicola (caap-a-goal)—   cured ham, can either be hot or sweet

Ceci (chee-chid-a) beans—   chick peas

Coffees (Caffe):

Caffe latte (caf-ay lot-tay)—   one part espresso to three parts steamed milk

Caffe macchiato (mah-chee-ah-toe)—	a shot of espresso with approximately 2 tablespoons of foamed milk
Caffe nocciola (no-ca-chee-oh-lah)—	hazelnut flavored coffee
Cappuccino (cop-a-chee-no)—	made up of 1/3 espresso, 1/3 steamed milk, 1/3 foamed milk
Espresso (x-press-oh)—	strong Italian coffee produced by forcing hot water under high pressure over finely ground coffee
Mochaccino (mo-kao-chee-no)—	hot chocolate, espresso and whipped cream

Foods Continued

Fen-oik—	fennel, tastes like licorice crunches like celery
Focaccia (fo-cah-chia)—	Italian flatbread
Frittata (frit-aht-tah)—	an Italian omelet, commonly potatoes or peppers and eggs
Frih-zail-a—	hard pretzel like bread with pepper or fennel
Ga-goots—	squash, also slang for idiot, nothing, "I ain't got ga-goots"
Garlic—	the "breath" of life for Italian Americans
Gelato (jell-ah-to)—	very creamy Italian ice cream
Genoa (gen-oh-ah) salami—	a medium spiced salami that originated in the Genoa area of Italy
Gorgonzola (gor-gon-zola)—	Italian blue-veined cheese
Grappa—	A strong alcoholic drink derived from the bottom of the wine vat, Italian moon shine
Gravy—	the real name for pasta red sauce, eaten every Sunday at about 2-3:00

Insalata (en-sah-lah-ta)— Italian for salad

Locatelli
(loke-ah-tell-ee)— a type of romano cheese made from sheep's milk

Marinara
(marr-in-ah-da)— NOT mair-in-air-a, red meatless sauce, consisting of tomatoes garlic and olive oil

Marsala (mar-sala)— sweet Italian dessert wine

Moretti— a type of Italian beer

Mortadella
(more-ta-dell-a)— pork flavored with peppercorns, olives, pistachios and garlic, the name comes from the mortar used to grind it

Mozzarella
(moot-sa-della)— firm white smooth mild flavored cheese, (can be wet or dry) found alone or in pizza, calzone. The "buffalo" (from buffalo milk) variety is best.

Olive oil— Italian Mother's milk. One of 2 essential ingredients to Italian American cooking. The other of course is garlic. Virgin olive oil has less than 1% acidity. It can be achieved technically or naturally.

Pancetta (pan-set-ta)— salted Italian bacon that comes from the belly of the pig

Parmesan (par-mah-jahn)— Italian hard cheese made from cow's milk

Pasta— see the pictorial pasta guide below

Pasta-a-maan-o— homemade pasta

Pasta fagioli
(pasta fa-zool)— pasta (ditalini) and thick bean soup. Great for gas

Pasta—fa-zeel— pasta soup (ditalini) with peas

Pasta len-teek— pasta (ditalini) soup with lentils. Good for New Years

Pasta ah-oi-ya— pasta with garlic and oil

Pellegrino— bottled water with gas (aqua con gas)

Peppers or potatoes
and eggs— good for lunch, dinner or anytime with or without

bread. Much later on I found that you command a handsome price for these if you call it a frittata.

Pepperoni— dried Italian ground beef and pork sausage, seasoned with pepper

Peroni— a type of Italian beer

Pesce (pae-sha)— fish

Pesto (pes-toe)— sauce consisting of basil, garlic, pine nuts and olive oil

Piccata (pi-cah-ta)— sauce made from lemon juice, capers and wine

Pignoli (pin-yo-lee)— pine nuts, little oval sweet nuts usually put in cookies or sometimes pasta

Pit-si-o— red sauce, pizza sauce

Polenta (pole-n-ta)— corn meal

Pomodoro (palm-ah-door-o)— tomato, sauce consisting of sauteed tomatoes, prosciutto and onions

Primavera (pree-mah-vare-a)— sauce made with mixed vegetables and tomato sauce

Prosciutto (pra-shuit)— cured ham (salt and air dried) from the hind leg of the pig, usually served in very thin slices

Provolone (pruv-ah-lone)— sharp, dry cow's milk cheese (the one that smells like feet)

Puttanesca (poot-ahn-esca)— "Poor mans sauce" made with anchovies, smells like fish or Puta. Puta is short for whore—you figure it out. I don't eat it.

Ricotta (ri-gaw-ta)— NOT rick-ott-a, Ricotta is a soft, slightly salty cheese similar to cottage cheese made from whey and used in a variety of pasta dishes.

Rigatoni ala Vodka— crème sauce with tomato, vodka (+/-) prosciutto

Rizzoto (riz-oh-toe)— dish made with rice, saffron, broth, onion and garlic

Romano (roe-mahn-oh)— hard Italian sheep's milk cheese, saltier than parmesan cheese

Salad—	lettuce with oil and vinegar
Sambuca (sam-buu-ca)—	anise flavored liqueur
Scungilli (scune-geel)—	conch
Semolina (sem-oh-leena)—	derived from durum wheat, it is used for making pasta. Its high fiber and protein content absorbs less water and gives pasta a chewy consistency
Sopressata (sou-pah-sahd)—	salami
Spa-dina—	rolled veal
Spumoni (spuu–moan-ee)—	Italian ice cream
Stromboli (strom-bo-lee)—	rolled stuffed pizza usually containing meat
Vino (vee-no)—	wine
Winge (win-je)—	taking a piece of bread and mopping it in the remaining sauce. Not in Miss Manner's book but worth looking like a pig.
Zucchini—	Italian summer squash
Zuppa (zuu-pah)—	soup

The pictorial pasta guide for pure paisans:

Pasta is the food of the gods. To Italian Americans it is synonymous with family. This is underscored by the fact that there is a pasta size and shape for just about every family member including seventh cousins. It has become the mainstay of our diet. My mother could reach into the refrigerator with her eyes closed, pull out the first thing she touched and mix it with pasta. She has mixed pasta with the likes of butter (now margarine of course), asparagus, beans, broccoli, cauliflower, eggs, escarole, garlic, oil, peas, squash, and of course other pasta. It never failed. Regardless of the size, shape or pasta partner it was always delicious. Because it is near impossible to keep up with the plethora of pastas, approximately 350, the following guide of the more common varieties was included for the true pasta purist to peruse.

Ancini di pepe (an-chee-nee dee-pep-pee), *peppercorns*

Cavatelli (cah-va-teil)

Conchiglie (con-keel-ee), *medium shells*

Cotelli or cavatappi, *elbow twists*

Ditalini (dee-tah-lee-nee), *little thimbles*

Farfalle (far-fah-lay), *butterflies, bow ties*

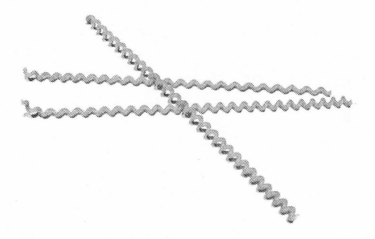

Fusilli (fu-zeel-ee), *spiral spaghetti*

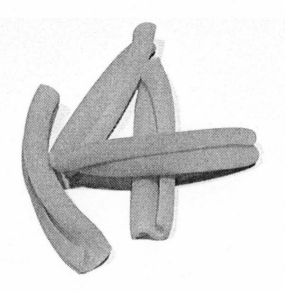

Gemelli (geh-mell-ee), *twins*

Gnocchi (in-yuk-ee) pasta

Gnocchi (in-yuk-ee), potato *dumplings*

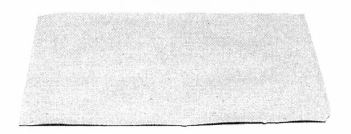

Lasagna/lasagne

Lasagnette

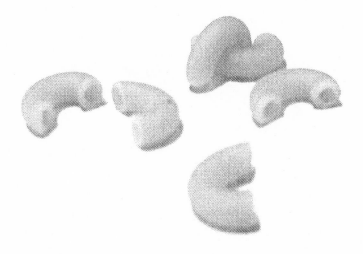

Macaroni

Manicotti (mahn-ih-gaut), *cannelloni in Italy, little muffs*

Mezzaluna (mez-ah-lu-na), *half moon*

Orecchiette (or-ech-ee-ette), *little ears*

Orzo (ort-zoe), *barley*

Pappardelle (pap-are-a-dell)

Fettucine

Linguine

Spaghetti

Capellini

Pasta pasta pasta in size order:
Cappellini (cap-elle-ee-nee) , *angel hair*
Vermicelli (ver-mih-chelle-ee), *little worms*
Spaghetti (spah-geh-tee), *strings*
Linguine (lin-gwee-nee), *little tongues*
Fettuccine (fet-uu-chee-nee), *little ribbons*

Penne (pen-ay), *feathers, quill pen*

Ravioli (rav-ee-oh-lee)

Rigatoni (rig-a-toe-nee), *large grooved*

Riso (ree-so)

Rotelli (roe-tell-ee), *wagon wheels*

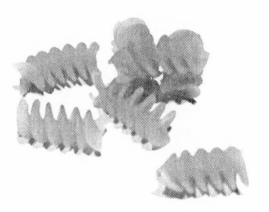

Rotini (ro-tee-nee), *spirals*

Sagnarelli (sag-nah-rell-ee)

Stellini (stell-ee-nee), *tiny stars*

Tagliatelle (tag-lee-a-tell)

Tortellini (tor-tell-ee-nee)

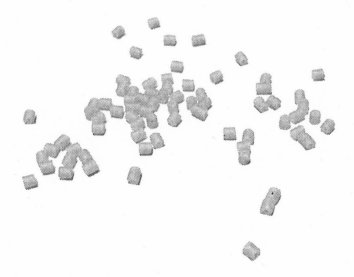

Tubettini (tube-ett-tee-nee), *little tubes*

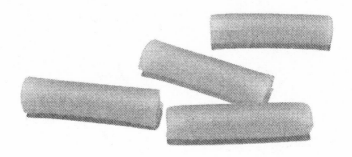

Ziti (zee-tee), *bridegrooms*

Songs for the heart

Nothing touches your heart or evokes memories like some of the famous songs performed by Italian Americans. These great artists were, and still are magical. They had the uncanny ability to evoke a multitude of emotions that transform you to another place and time. To this day, just one verse of "Mala Femmina" brings me back to my mother's kitchen on Sunday morning. I can still hear the sound of miniature fireworks exploding as meatballs fry for the family dinner that afternoon. As she glides with neurosurgical precision through the kitchen, my mother whispers the words and hums those few Italian phrases she's forgotten. And if you ever want to see a room full of "tough guys" put on a show, play "Mama" at a wedding after about two glasses of Chianti. There won't be enough napkins (tough guys don't use tissues).

On the other hand, many of these songs were also invigorating and had the mystical effect of Tarzan or the Pied Piper. The entrancing sound of the Tarantella (tarantula) at a wedding would cause many of my relatives to get up off their normally sedentary "coolies" and move their much more than Rubinesque torsos to the dance floor. There they would bounce, hop and move their feet, untiring, with Christmas morning smiles. Then uncle Roberto would get up, the half chewed, unlit stogie hanging from his lip like an extra appendage to sing "Che la luna" to the crowd. Like good wine, these songs can be stored on the shelf and sampled on those special occasions.

Finally, while a few other ethnic groups may claim fame to emotional classics similar to Amore, Volare, Innamorata and O Sole Mio, no body and I mean "no botty" else has given us masterpieces like "Pepino the Italian Mouse", "Dominic the Christmas Donkey" and who can forget "Mama Get a Hammer There's a Fly on Papa's Head". My mother used to say, "what doesn't make you laugh, doesn't make you cry". Right again Ma!

The masters of Italian American song:

Tony Bennett
Enrico Caruso
Perry Como
Pat Cooper
Vic Damone
Connie Francis
Julius LaRosa
Dean Martin
Al Martino
Domenico Modugno
Lou Monte
Louis Prima
Frank Sinatra
Jerry Vale

Music that fills your heart and your eyes:

Al di la
Amore
Amore Scusami
Angelina
Arrivederci Roma (good bye to Rome)
Bella Ciao

Buona Sera

Chia

Ciao Ciao Bambina

Come Back To Sorrento

Domani

Dominick the Christmas Donkey

For Mama

Funiculi funicula

Hey Gumbaree

Innamorata (sweetheart)

La Tarantella

Lazy Mary (Che-la-luna)

Love Theme From the "Godfather"

Mala Femmina

Mama

Marina

Mattinata

Mama Get A Hammer There's a Fly On Papa's Head

Non Dimenticar (don't forget)

Oh Marie

O Sole Mio

Papa Loves Mombo

Pepino The Italian Mouse

Return To Me

Russella E. Maggio

Santa Lucia

Shaddup You Face

Soldi, Soldi, Soldi

Traviata—Italian Drinking Song

Volare (Nel Blu Dipinto Di Blu)

Movies:

There are a plethora of Italian American movies that have been produced. Once again, this may be related to the fact that as a people, Italian Americans are characters. They are unique, cheerful, colorful, animated and amusing. This sells. These movies demonstrate the myriad of personalities found in the Italian American community. Often considered stereotypical, they commonly contain that certain grain of truth that can generate a memory, a smile and maybe a tear.

A Bronx Tale
A Godfather's Story
A Streetcar Named Desire
Analyze This
Angie
Bella Mafia
Bugsy
Casino
China Girl
Cookie
Donnie Brasco
Fatso
Federal Hill
Gangster Wars
Get Shorty
Goodfellas
Gotti
Honor Thy Father
Household Saints
Johnny Stecchino

Italians in America
Italianamerican / The Big Shave
La Dolce Vita
Lansky
Last Don
Love With a Proper Stranger
Mac
Mafia
Mafia Cop
Mafia Dynasty
Married to the Mob
Marty
Mean Streets
Mickey Blue Eyes
Mobsters
Moonstruck
Murder Incorporated
My Cousin Vinny
Our Contributions: The Italians in America
Prizzi's Honor
Raging Bull
Rocky
Saturday Night Fever
Scarface
Spike of Bensonhurst
The Freshman
The Gang That Couldn't Shoot Straight
The Godfather Trilogy
The Last Don
The Lost Capone
True Love
The Rose Tattoo
Wise Guys
Witness to the Mob

How "THE BOYS" say it

Throughout history, no matter how regal an empire, how benevolent a nation or how altruistic a society, a sub culture or dark side commonly existed within. This is also true of Italian American culture. Appropriate or not, the Mafioso, La Cosa Nostra and organized crime have unfortunately been synonymous with Italian Americans. Regrettably, this blackens the eye of many immigrants and their families who are respectable and hard working individuals. Especially since, there were, and are, many other ethnic groups involved in the business of organized crime. Maybe they just lack the romantic Italian names, charisma and animated persona that has been sensationalized by the media for profit. Regardless, this illicit group of individuals often uses a unique jargon. Because of the current media fascination with these individuals, no guide would be complete without definitions of some of their commonly used words and phrases.

Ace of Diamonds—	the hard luck card, after the mob hit of Joe Masseria when the ace of diamonds dangled from his cold stiff just murdered hand
Administration—	management level positions in "the family". This usually includes the boss, underboss and consigliere
American Mafia—	a group of criminals organized into families
Associates—	players (work for the mob) who can't be "made" because they lack an Italian father
Bagman—	mobsters who carried cash for bribes
Black Hand—	some equate this with the Mafia, they were extortionists in the Little Italy's of the US who would either take your money or your life. They signed the extortion with a Black Hand . This ran out of favor with the advent of fingerprinting
Boss—	the head of the family
Bringing both sets—	when a mobster brings his wife and mistress to the same event
Bums—	people who were recipients of a hit
Business associate—	member of organized crime
Buttlegging—	selling untaxed cigarettes acquired from another state without taxes
Capo—	short for capodecina or caporegime, captain of a crew or decina a group of 10—15 soldiers
Capo-di-tutti-capo—	boss of all bosses
Buttonmen—	soldiers
Clean graft—	money to police officers for overlooking vices like prostitution

Clip—	to murder
Comare—	mistress, girlfriend aka goomah
Commission—	heads (Bosses) of the families that set policy and settle interfamily disputes for La Cosa Nostra
Compare—	the emotional tie between Italians
Confirm—	to become a "made" member of the mob
Consigliere—	lawyer, advisor, counselor, negotiator
Coperegima—	captain
Contract—	business contract for murder, the person ordering it was often 3 or 4 times removed from the hit
Crew—	group of soldiers in a family under the command of a capo
Cugine—	soldier trying to get made
Dirty graft—	drug money
Don—	title of respect, not really a position in the Mafia hierarchy, however, it is often interpreted that way
Fell off the truck—	stolen or hijacked goods. Hey where did you get those? They fell off the truck.
Friend of mine—	just connected not yet made
Friend of ours—	made man
G—	a thousand dollars
Garbage business—	see private carting
Going heavy—	carrying a weapon (aka carrying)
Goombah—	a paisan, friend, officially someone who is a helper
Goomah—	mafia mistress
Heavy—	packing, carrying a weapon
Hijacker—	hitman
Hit—	to murder
Ice pick murders—	a favorite weapon that was massaged to an art form. Strategically placed ice pick through the ear drum into the brain made the death look like it was from natural causes. The ice pick could also be used numerous times as a "message" kill.

Kiss of death—	kiss on the lips as a warning or indication of danger
La Cosa Nostra—	"this thing of ours", the Mob, the Outfit, the Syndicate. Actually a word overheard by the FBI while the Mob was being bugged. J. Edgar Hoover made it popular to save his butt because he had previously denied the existence of the Mafia.
Large—	thousand, as in 50 large (50 thousand)
La Tuna—	a federal correction institution famous for housing Mafia stool pigeons
Lieutenant—	rank in the mob, below capo
Little Joe—	taken from dice, 2 rows of 2. Aka a method of execution leaving 2 rows of 2 bullet holes for loansharks, debtors and people who didn't pay up.
Made man—	when someone becomes an official member of the family. The Mafia reportedly has a secret ceremony for this but in reality this probably doesn't exist.
Mafia—	aka outfit, syndicate, arm, office, mob, Unione. Some possible derivations of the word Mafia: Derived from an arabic word for refuge. A Sicilian adjective for courage strength and endurance. Acronym for Morte Alla Franciese Italia Annella—"Death to the French is Italy's cry". From when the French occupied Italy. "My daughter", ma fia, allegedly a unifying cry when a French soldier in Palermo raped a young Italian girl. Mother and Father Italian Association
Mafia coffin—	used in the past, a double decker or false bottomed coffin. The slain victim is placed beneath a legitimate corpse and buried.
Mafioso—	Mafia
Mattresses—	aka "hitting the mattresses". Going to the mattresses refers to a gang war where the mafiosa stay together to fight the battle. During the war the members often hole

up in empty places with mattresses which serve as a place to sleep as well as a shield on the windows and doors during a gun battle.

Message job— strategically placing a bullet so that a message is left to the survivors

Moe Green special— being whacked with a gun shot to the eye

Mortadella— see under food, slang for loser

Murder Incorporated— this was a choice multinational group of executioners who could be hired by other mobsters to kill, whack or hit. Located in Brooklyn they could be hired for anywhere in the US. They could not be employed for hitting politicians or journalists. They broke up around 1940.

Muscle— strong arming, bullying, to influence someone, or a group of tough guys

Mustache Petes— The old guard Mafia from Italy early in the 1900's. They were eliminated by the new guard during prohibition.

O-merta— translated as honor, the golden rule of the mafia, oath of secrecy loyalty Pay-rolla—your "word"

Peddler— aka shoveler, one who disposes of the bodies

Pinched— to be caught by the law

Plants— "sleepers" these are people in the mob that remain crime free and lead normal lives (hopefully influential in business, labor or politics) until needed

Private carting— not just garbage but a semi-legitimate way to produce lots of lire. Not just for anyone, however, as it is allegedly controlled by organized crime.

Rat— someone who squeals, stool pigeon

RICO act— an acronym for Racketeer Influenced and Corrupt Organizations, passed in 1970 to crack down on organized crime but applied mainly after 1980 after the courts closed the appropriate loopholes. After this, stiff sentences could be applied to organized crime, but even worse, illicit proceeds and wealth related to these crimes could be seized.

Shylock— loanshark

Sicilian flu— a false illness that was feigned to prevent a mobster from being arrested or imprisoned

Sit down— a meeting among members of the Mafia—usually to settle differences

Skipper— head of a crew

Sleeping with the fish— drowned, dead

Soldier— a lower member of the Cosa Nostra, mob

So long pal— a mob farewell (at funerals)

Stand in— a lower ranked mobster that took the rap, or prison sentence for a higher ranked mobster. Usually done for money or elevation of status.

Stand up guy— one who doesn't talk or rat to the authorities despite the pressure or deal

Taken for a ride— intended victim of a hit is taken for a ride in a vehicle while the assailant in the back seat puts a gun to his head and fires

The boys— a nice way of referring to organized crime members

The family— a nice way to refer to organized crime family especially ones who are close

The old country— Italy

The other side— Italy

Tough guy— MOM—member of the mob

Underboss— second in command, CEO, makes sure that orders are carried out

Upped— to get elevated in rank in the mob hierarchy

Whack— to kill somebody

Wise guy— "made" member of the mob

Vendetta— feud

Not so nice-a words

The faint hearted might just as well skip this chapter. Some of these words may be offensive, however, I included them since they were the first Italian American words I was exposed to and learned. Everybody used them, my Aunts, my Uncles, the Jewish kid next door. No one was exempt. My Aunt Rosie could rattle off a tirade of expletives telling someone that they could put something, someplace in one of their relatives and it sounded like a sonata. It was an art. The way I see it, Italian Americans are an expressive people. This was just another form of expression. Since many of these words have been exploited in Italian American movies, I felt the book would be incomplete without them. Once again, a few of these words uttered strategically during a bocce game can disguise the fact that you know absolutely no Italian.

Ah fah-to matz	
ay-zor-ta-da—	up your sister's behind
Ah-vay-say	
mom-ah-da—	your mother's anatomy
Bach-a-la—	a smelly fish, slang for idiot, or part of the female anatomy
Bag-as-see-a—	b*tch, whore
Chooch—	slow and dumb person, literally a donkey
Col-uunes—	male private parts
Cor-nu-to—	bastard, sh*t
Cu-la-teen-a—	homosexual
Don-cheech—	the head chooch (see chooch)
Dra-jewel—	big, slow, dumb oaf
Fah-cha bru-tah—	ugly face
Fah-cha bob-ah-da—	face like a duck
Fah-nob-ah-la—	go to Naples, go to Hell
Fan-oik—	literally fennel, slang for gay
Fon-gool—	loosely means "F" yourself, sometimes used as baah— fon-gool
Frigg-in—	a euphemism or more acceptable way of saying the "F" word. To reduce the perceived vulgarity, frig or friggin can be used in its place. For example, at weddings, funerals or Broadway shows.
The "F" word—	the signature word for some Italian Americans, no longer restricted to short tempered males. With skill, it can be placed anywhere in a sentence and used as any form of grammar. Commonly used for effect like; what the "F", you're "F'in" kidding, get the "F" oudda heeh, or hey "F" face to name a few. It can also be complimentary. It's "F" ing buu-tee-ful. Real clever individuals can actually place it within a word!! Im-"F" ing-pressive!!!

Gavone—	crude, rude, backward, Italian American without manners
Geep—	crude, rude, backward, Italian American without manners
Gool—	backside
Gool-ay-zor-ta-da—	your sister's backside
Gotz—	male anatomy
Gyac—ya—doan—	someone who talks too much, someone you want to avoid
Jam-ook—	idiot
Kay-brute—	how ugly
Lon-use-a—	a useless individual
Lum-bree-own—	a big oaf
Lo-fa—	fart
Ma-luke—	dopey
Mear-da—	sh*t
Ming—	sh*t but in a way to express anger or surprise
Mor-ta-dell-a—	a type of sausage, slang for loser
Mool-in-yaahn—	eggplant, a disparaging term for African Americans
Moosh-a-vase—	slow, lethargic
Moo-tee-vahm—	someone with a ravenous appetite who doesn't mind displaying it, pig like
Noz-ee-bra-chole—	nose like a braciole
Ooo-gots—	male anatomy
Pa-kwak—	female anatomy
Pish-a-zote—	piss the pants
Poot-ana—	whore
Por-ko—	pig
Rat—bastid—	common derogatory expression of unknown meaning and origin
Shum-in-eed—	dopey, stupid
Ski-foosa—	someone that disgusts you, ugly woman

Son-a-ma-bitch—	Italian American way of saying son of a bitch
Stuu-nod—	stupid, in a stupor
Strunz—	crap, sh*t
Strunz eh med—	sh*t head
Stu-gotz—	male anatomy
Sva-cheeme—	everybody uses it, nobody knows the definition, but it is bad
Tette—	breast
Whoo-er—	whore
Zing-ah-da—	dresses like a rag, sloppy, gypsy

Geno, don't leave home without these!

Irrespective of political correctness, there are certain attributes of Italian Americans that make them stand out in a game of "where's Mario". These characteristics, often considered stereotypes, include physical appearance, manner of speech, attire and religious practices. Realistically these "stereotypes" are simply similar traits and traditions that have endured among people with a common background. Over time with the Americanization of the old ways many of these typifying features have been diluted. Despite this, it is hard to deny that there are those defining features that still say "now that's Italian". For example, if you see a person with curly dark hair, a big bushy mustache, dressed in black with hands gesturing wildly as they speak. Who comes to mind? You guessed it. She's Italian. The following section deals with those things (stereotypes) that many Italian Americans still adhere to, that distinguish them from everyone else. The same things that differentiated me from Danny Cruz, Joe Kempski, Henry Berberich, Robert Friedman and the rest of the kids in my multinational neighborhood.

To begin with, most Italian Americans are somewhat religious. I say somewhat because most consider themselves religious, at least according to their own interpretation. Uncle Tony believed he was absolved of all sins as long as Aunt Filly went to church every Sunday. Also, a few strategically timed signs of the cross were always good for a few divine brownie points. Of course, the other extreme also exists—those who went to Mass every Sunday as well as Christmas Eve, Good Friday, Holy Thursday and All Saint's Day. And if you were really devout, TV mass every day. Till this day, every time my mother passes a church of any denomination she reflexively makes the sign of the cross. With the plethora of new churches that have popped up this can be an onerous task. Some of my Jewish friends who rode with my mother for the first time were convinced she had a tic. Regardless, most Italian Americans will say they are religious whether or not they practice the traditional dogma.

Here lies the dichotomy. Despite their steadfast religious beliefs, many Italian Americans are very superstitious. Along with these superstitions come objects or talismans that theoretically can protect them and ward off evil spirits. First off, everyone must have the Virgin Mary displayed in one form or another. The Virgin Mary is probably the most prolific of all religious objects and she can be found in a myriad of designs. For starters she can be made of concrete, porcelain, wood, gold, silver or oil paint to name a few. She can be found in the garden (Mary in the shell), hung on the wall, displayed on furniture, or worn around the neck. It has always been appropriate to keep some rendition of her in the master bedroom. Her presence protects and safeguards both property and physical well being. She is worshipped unequivocally. Italian American women idolize her because she is the quintessential mother. Italian American men idolize her because she is symbolic of their mother.

In addition to the Virgin Mother there are at least three other items that Italian Americans believe possess that miraculous ability to avert evil and harbor good fortune. Most importantly they are supposed to protect one from the "mal-oik-ya". This is better known as the evil eye, essentially a curse or spell for bad luck. One is especially susceptible to the mal-oik-ya if they just crossed someone, are financially successful or have just purchased a flashy high-ticket item. Although the process of spitting in the air with an audible "tuu" has a similar avoidance of the evil eye, it obviously doesn't have the same lasting power of a charm. The most common charm used to avoid this curse is the ubiquitous Italian horn. Basically, this looks like a pepper, comes in many sizes and is commonly made of gold, silver or plastic. It is usually worn as a necklace but the plastic variety, always red, can be hung anywhere. It is not uncommon to see these hanging from a car's rear view mirror. Since it has become so commercialized, the horn, can occasionally be found on the necklaces of other ethnic groups. However, one thing is for certain, if the horn is made of gold, really big and gaudy, the bearer is Italian American.

Like the Italian horn, but not as prevalent is the Italian hand. It too wards off the evil eye. In fact, it is a miniature replica of the finger positioning necessary to deliver the mal-oik-ya. Obviously, if the mal-oik-ya can be received, it can also be administered. The third and fourth fingers are folded down and the pinky and forefinger pointed forward. Then with a quick forward motion this hand is jabbed in the direction of the person or thing to which the mal-oik-ya is cast. It is commonly accompanied by a grunt or expletive. Hypothetically, a likeness of the Italian hand, worn around the neck or hung in a strategic place will immunize one from receiving the evil vibes should this action be directed their way.

In addition to the horn and hand the red ribbon has also been used to protect new purchases from the evil eye. After any major extravagant purchase, especially a car or home, it was essential to discretely hang a red ribbon bow somewhere within. Most commonly this was in the attic of the home and the rear view mirror of the car. We always kept red ribbon on hand in case of emergency. God forbid you drove off in that new car without the red ribbon force field.

There are two other items that are common to Italian Americans for divine protection and instant spiritual communication. The first of these is that old cross shaped piece of palm received at a past Palm Sunday. You didn't necessarily have to go to church yourself to receive it but at least carrying or displaying it gave you a layer of almighty protection. The other watts line to God used by many Italian Americans is the mass card of a prominent family member, usually a parent or grandparent. In times of trouble or despair this could be whipped out of the wallet or purse and provide you with an instant hot line to God.

Besides religious items there is certain apparel that tends to distinguish many Italian Americans from other ethnic groups. It is no secret that many of us love gold. It is as if the more vowels you have in your name the more gold you are supposed to wear. Conveniently, this precious metal can be displayed in a variety of fashions. Very commonly it is worn as a necklace with or without one or more medals. It can be discreet or it can look like a room at the Vatican. The necklace is often complemented with a gold bracelet and a pinky ring to complete the ensemble. For many

Italian Americans gold is just another mineral with a recommended daily allowance. Fortunately, it is non-toxic, except perhaps to the onlooker.

Another bit of attire often found in the dresser of Italian American men is the tank top tee shirt. Disparagingly, this has also been referred to as the "Guinea tee" or down south as the "wife beater tee". This simple tee shirt conveys a hierarchy of culture. The most regal Italian Americans keep the tee tucked away in the back of a drawer in case of an emergency. Then and only then it is worn discreetly beneath a shirt. For the middle class of this fashion hierarchy it is acceptable to don the tee, by itself, around the house, especially on days off. Finally, there are those, commonly referred to as gavones or geeps, who consider the tee shirt stylish enough to wear in the yard, at the mall or even at a professional baseball game. They never have to worry because the wardrobe is always the same. The biggest obstacle for these guys is keeping the spaghetti sauce out of their chest hair.

The other extreme are the Rudolf Valentinos. These are the guys who seem to have lost the first three buttons of every shirt they own. Their chests are reminiscent of the bow of the Titanic as it parts the oncoming sea. Many chests, of course come complete with a glaring gold anchor or its equivalent. Why many Italian American males find it imperative to keep the upper part of their shirt unbuttoned remains an enigma. As far as I can figure, some of us spend so much energy adjusting ourselves that we are just too tired to finish buttoning our shirts. Go figure.

I guess one of the final common denominators among those that stand out as Italian American stereotypes is that sheen that seems to emanate from our locks. I am not sure why we glisten. At one point I was convinced it was because some of us maintained a toxic olive oil blood level. It was so bad during my puberty that I considered selling the oil rights of my hair to Exxon. To make matters worse, some of us now add insult to injury by spit shining our hair with "gel". It's like olive oil in a can. I guess you might equate the application of hair gel to a salvo of exclamation points at the end of the sentence—you're damn right I'm Italian!!!!!!!!!!!

You can't deny you're a paisan if...

Your last name contains more vowels than consonants.

When entering Ellis Island your great uncle changed his name from Caridi to Carridi so it wouldn't sound Italian.

None of your aunts are taller than 5 feet or weigh less than 250 pounds.

You have actually used the word "chooch" in a sentence.

You eat things with tentacles and suction cups at least once a year, usually Christmas Eve.

Christmas Eve is a bigger event than Christmas Day.

You consider yourself religious but haven't been to mass since they spoke Latin.

You wear a gold chain with at least 2 medals one of which is an Italian horn or hand.

Your richest relatives are in the garbage business.

You subconsciously adjust yourself 230 times each hour.

Your cousin's wedding had more chins than a Chinese phone book.

You only see your aunts at weddings and funerals. The rest of the time your uncles travel with their female "business partners".

You never bought a pack of cigarettes that had a tax stamp on it.

At your family's weddings and funerals there were always well-dressed guys who were interested in your license plate.

You not only know how to dance the Tarantella, you know what it means.

More than 4 of your relatives have broken their nose.

You have 5 cousins with the same name.

You have family members that still march in the Columbus Day parade.

Your mother said there is no such thing as the Mafia.

A 70 year old aunt you haven't seen in ten years comes up to you and asks "oooo, how the "F" are you" ?

During puberty your sister had a better mustache than any of your friends.

Your family needs a truckload of tissues at a wedding or funeral.

Your senior citizen aunts and uncles still call you Jamesy.

You have a 5-foot, 300-pound aunt nicknamed "cookie".

All of your uncle's middle names are in parentheses.

You never use the word sauce, only gravy.

You hate the moronic commercials for chain food Italian restaurants depicting stereotypical patrons actually enjoying microwave pasta concoctions.

You have eaten at least 5 different pasta dishes that contained a different vegetable each time.

At your wedding you only received cash gifts, it was put in a bag (a boost) and was enough for a house down payment.

Your mother uses expressions like "maah-done".

On Christmas Eve, the dining room table has more fish than the local aquarium.

You're a 50-year-old man and you can't listen to the song "Mama" without crying. And your mother is alive.

Twenty teary eyed family members come to the hospital with you when you get your routine chest x-ray.

You know the names and can identify at least 10 different types of pasta.

You know the words to the song "Shaddup You Face".

There is an Italian flag somewhere in the house.

Your grandfather poured wine from a gallon jug over his shoulder into a glass.

You have a statue of the Virgin Mary in the master bedroom or in the garden.

Your mother has a set of Rosary beads under her pillow or in her bra.

You know where the name puttanesca sauce comes from.

You have to shave your lower neck. Just like your brother.

You have no idea that you are missing the first 3 buttons on all your dress shirts.

Nobody has ever sat in Aunt Tilley's living room and the furniture is covered with plastic. Not too mention it's also lime green.

None of your mother's family has a neck.

You know how to pronounce marinara and mozzarella.

You have eaten at least three different types of ham or salami and know their names.

You have not only played bocce but you also know the rules.

Somebody you know is a gavone.

You drank wine with your grandfather before you were 10 years old.

You know what anisette tastes like and still drink it.

You have that one lucky uncle who constantly finds expensive stuff that falls off a truck.

You have an Uncle Jimmy whose real name is Vincent.

There was one table at your wedding where everyone had to sit facing the door.

You own at least 4 black shirts.

You can fit at least 3 fingers in one nostril.

You keep 3 spare bottles of hair gel in case of emergency.

You have given someone or something the "mal-oik-ya".

Your Aunt Nunzi's bikini wax extends to her belly button.

You never think food has too much garlic.

You've been to the feast of San Gennaro.

At least one of your grandparents used to say "son-a-ma-b*tch".

You have made struffoli and eaten zeppola.

Your CD collection includes Eh Paisano and others by Lou Monte, Louie Prima, Perry Como and Dean Martin.

Your family owns stock in Gillette, Schick and Nair.

You really do have an Aunt Filly.

You thought your nose was normal size until you started grade school.

Your front license plate is an Italian flag design.

You are proud of your Italian American heritage.

Festa Italiana

Nothing beats an Italian festival. The aroma of fresh fried zeppole waft through the air as throngs of reveling sponges soak up the endless array of food, wine and music. Fortunately for us, there are a myriad of Italian festivals held throughout the country for one reason or another. Some pay homage to a Saint or hero while others simply pay tribute to the Italian American heritage. They all have the same common theme, however, family, friendship, food and fun. Most festivals occur in or around summer and Columbus Day. Since it would be impossible to stay current with the exact dates, I have included the cities in which Italian festivals have occurred most commonly. The exact dates and times may be available through the chamber of commerce or the Internet.

California

Jackson—Sutter Creek	Italian Society Picnic
Lodi	Festa Italiana
Monterey	Santa Rosalia Festival
Oakland	Festa
Oak Park	Italian Festa
Sacramento	Italian Festival
San Diego	Columbus Day Festa
	Italian Streetpainting Festival
San Jose	Italian Family Festival
San Luis Obispo	Italian Street painting festival
San Rafael	Italian Street painting festival
Santa Barbara	Italian Street painting festival

	Italian Festa
Santa Rosa	Festa Italiana
Visalia	Putignana—Visalia sister City Italian Festival

Colorado

Denver	Feast of St. Rocco

Connecticut

Ansonia	Italian Festa
New Haven	Feast of St. Anthony
	Feast of Santa Maria Maddalena
Norwich	The Taste of Italy
Stafford	Italian Picnic
Waterbury	San Donato Festa
Westport	Festival Italiano

Delaware

Wilmington	St. Anthony's Italian American Festival

Florida

Ft. Walton Beach	Festa Italiana
Gainesville	Chooch Fest
Melbourne	Italian Feast of Florida
Palm Coast	Festa
Venice	Italiana Feast and Carnival
Vero Beach	Columbus Day Fest
Ybor City	Festa Italiana

Illinois

Benold	Italian American Days
Blue Island	Street Festival, Carnival
Chicago Heights	Feast of St. Lorenzo
Chicago-Melrose Park	Our Lady of Mt. Carmel Festival
Chicago-North Lake	Villa Day
Chicago	Heart of Italy Food and Wine Festival
	St. Joseph Festival
Societa San Giovanni Bosco	Di. Ciminna
	Feast of San Rocco Di Potenza
	Feast of Maria Santissima Lauretana
	Feast of St. Donatus
Farmington	Italian Festa
Herrin	Herrinfesta Italiana
Rockford	Festa Italiana
Stone Park	Italian Cultural Center Italian Day Picnic
	Feast of St. Beato Giovanni Liccio di Caccamo
	Feast of St. Francesco di Paola

Indiana

Clinton	Little Italy Festival
Indianapolis	Italian Street Festival

Iowa

Des Moines	Festa Italiana

Kentucky

Louisville	Festa Italiana
Newport	Italianfest

Louisiana

Harvey	St. Rosalie Parish Fair
Independence	Independence Italian Festival
New Orleans	Maria Santissima Della Favara Feast
	Italian Marching Parade

Maine

North Adams	June Fest Italian Street Fair
Portland	St Rocco's Street Bazaar

Massachusetts

Boston	Madona Del Grazie
	San Antonio Di Padova Da Montefalcione Inc.
	Italia Unita's Annual Italian Festival
Cambridge	Annual Italian Feast of Saints Cosmas and Damian—Patrons of Gaeta, Italy
East Boston	Italian Festival
Lawrence	Feast of the Three Saints
Worcester	Feast of Our Lady of Mt. Carmel

Michigan

Grand Rapids	Festa Italiana
Sterling Heights	Italian Festival at Freedom Hill Park

Minnesota

Chisholm	Festa Italiana

Missouri

Saint Louis	Columbus Day Parade and Festival

Nebraska

Omaha	La Festa Italiana

Nevada

Reno	Eldorado's Italian Festival

New Jersey

Bayonne	Italian Carnival
East Rutherford	Festa Italiana
Hammonton	Feast of Mt. Carmel
Hoboken	Monte San Giacomo Cultural Festival
	St. Ann's Italian/American Street Festival
	Monte San Giacomo Cultural Festival
Holmdel	Italian Heritage Festival
Lodi	St. Joseph
Long Branch	Sons of Italy Italian Festival
North Wildwood	Italian American Weekend
Oakhurst	Italian American Festival
West Windsor	Mercer County Italian American Festival

New York

Bronx	St. Anthony Feast
	Mt. Carmel Feast
	Our Lady of Mount Carmel
Brooklyn	Feast of the Giglio
Buffalo	Sorrento Cheese Italian Heritage Festival
Glen Cove	Feast of St. Rocco
	Tomato Festival
Hempstead	Hofstra University Italian Festival
Manhattan	San Gennaro Festival
Massapequa	Long Island Giglio Assoc. Feast of the Giglio
Scotia	Capital Region Festa Italiana
Syracuse	Festa Italiana
Utica	Festival of Saints Cosmos and Damian
Valhalla	Italian Festival
Watertown	Mt. Carmel Italian Religious Festival
	Bravo Italiano Festival
Westbury	Feast of Madonna Dell'Assunta

Oklahoma

McAlester	Italian Festival

Ohio

Canton	Canton Italian American Festival
Cleveland	Feast of the Assumption
Columbus	The Columbus Italian Festival
Cuyahoga Falls	Italian American Festival
Lowellville	Our Lady of Mt. Carmel Festa

New Philadelphia	Tuscarawas County Itailan-American Festival
Youngstown	L'il Italy Feast

Oregon

Portland	Festa Italiana

Pennsylvania

Aliquippa	Festa di San Rocco
Crabtree	Feast of Our Lady of Mt. Carmel
Dunmore	St. Rocco's Italian Feast
Easton	Tempo Italiano
Erie	St. Joseph's Day
	Italian Festival
	Italian American Day Picnic
	Festival of the Assumption
	St. Paul's festival
	Mazzini Civic Ass. Italian American Picnic
Old Forge	Elittese Festival
Pittsburgh	Festa Italia
	Columbus Day Parade
Scranton	Italian Festival

Rhode Island

Newport	Festa Italiana
Westerly	Mt. Carmel Feast

South Carolina

Fort Mill	Festa Italiana

Tennessee

Memphis	Memphis Italian Festival
Nashville	Italian Street Fair

Texas

Houston	Festa Italiana
Austin	Annual Festa Italian

Washington

Seattle	Festa Italiana
Walla Walla	Fourteen Italian Heritage Days Festa & Parade
Washington, DC	Festa Italiana

West Virginia

Clarksburg	Italian Heritage Festival
Wheeling	Ohio Valley Italian Festival

Wisconsin

Kenosha	Feast of Our Lady of the Holy Rosary
	Our Lady of Mt. Carmel Festival
Milwaukee	Feasta Italiana

Exploring
Italian American Web Sites

In keeping with the "guide" aspect of "Yo Capeesh", I felt compelled to include a listing of the useful and informative Italian American web sites found on the Internet. As opposed to books, these sites are dynamic and have the ability to remain current. Each one of these sites has its own merit and can be used to further explore the realm of Italian Americana.

There is, however, a caveat. Because of the current tide of political correctness and some of the on-the-edge material contained in this book, I am solely responsible for the contents of "Yo Capeesh". The following web sites did not review nor condone the elements contained within this book. They have no knowledge of the contents and are not related in any way. These sites were simply included by me to help interested readers expound upon the Italian American experience.

American Italian Historical Association
   mobilito.com/aiha

American Italian Renaissance Foundation
   www.airf.org/pages/organizations

Bella Italia Mia, Inc
   expage.com/page/bellaitaliamia

Bocce Links
   home.netcom.com/~mifisher/bocce

Collegiate Italian American Organization
    www.geocities.com/ciaoatpaceuniversity

Cyber Italian
    www.cyberitalian.com

Dance of the Giglio Feasts
    www.giglio-usa.org

Ellis Island
    www.ellisisland.org

Feast of San Gennaro
    www.littleitalynyc.com/sg_page1.asp

Ferrara Café
    www.ferraracafe.com/?littleitalynyc

Festa Italiana Portland Oregon
    www.festa-italiana.org

Festa Italiana Ybor City
    www.festaitalianatampa.com

FIERI International
    www.fieri.org

Guide to Italian American Clubs and Organizations
    www.itconnect.net/clubs.htm

Herrinfesta Italiana Illinois
    www.herrinfesta.com/pages/herrinfesta.php

Historical Society of W. Pennsylvania Italian Americans
   wpaitalians.com

I Love Pasta.org
   www.ilovepasta.org

Italiamerica
   www.italiamerica.org

Italiamerica Book Store
   www.italiamerica.org/books

Italian American Bookshelf
   www.italianamericanbooks.com

Italiamia
   www.italiamia.com

Italian American Brotherhood Club
   www.northeastohio.com/iabc/home.htm

Italian American Assn. of Ocean Township NJ
   www.iaato.com

Italian American Connection
   www.theitalianamericanconnection.com

Italian American Cultural Society of El Paso
   www.italianclubs.com

Italian American Heritage Foundation
   iahfsj.org

Italian American History: A Timeline
pirate.shu.edu/~connelwi/itamtime.htm

Italian American Homepage
members.aol.com/AlSkor/italo-amer.html

Italian Americans
www.holycross.edu/departments/history/

Italian Americans.com
www.italianamericans.com

Italian Americans in the News
www.geocities.com/rdenapoli/news.html

Italian American Lawyers Assn.
www.iala.lawzone.com

Italian American Marching Club of New Orleans
italianamericanmarchingclub.com

Italian American Museum
italianamericanmuseum.org

Italian American Police Society of New Jersey
www.iapsnj.org

Italian American Webring
http://www.angelfire.com/ny/maryg/ring.html

Italianamericans web site
www.italianamericans.com/home.htm

Italian American Web Site of New York
   www.italian-american.com

Italian American Writers
   italianamericanwrtiters.com

Italian Ancestry
   www.italianancestry.com

Italian Club of Little Rock Arkansas
   www.aristotle.net/~dianag

Italian Club of Tampa
   www.italian-club.org

Italian Cultural Center of Greater Austin
   www.austinitalians.org

Italian Festival of McAlester OK
   www.italianfestival.org

Italian Festivals
   www.italylink.com/festivals.html

Italian Food.com
   italianfood.com

Italian Genealogy
   www.daddezio.com

Italian Heritage.net
   italianheritage.net

Italian Historical Society of America
italianhistorical.org

Italian Info
www.italianinfo.net/

Italian Novelties
www.italiannovelties.com

Italian Wine Club
www.italianwineclub.biz

Italian Sinfonia
geocities.com/italianmusic

Italians in the States
italiansinthestates.com

Italians of America Cultural Society North Denver
www.italiansofamerica.com

Italiansrus.com
italiansrus.com

Italy at St. Louis
www.italystl.com

John D. Calandra Italian American Institute
www.qc.edu/calandra/index.html

L'Italo-Americano
www.italoamericano.com/index.htm

Little Italy MD
   www.littleitalymd.com

Little Italy NYC
   www.littleitalynyc.com

Little Italy San Diego
   www.littleitalysd.com/splash/index.asp

Loggia Glen Cove
   www.loggiaglencove.org/osialodg.htm

My Italian Family.com
   www.myitalianfamily.com

My Paisan.com
   www.mypaisan.com

National Italian American Bar Association
   niaba.org

National Italian American Foundation
   www.niaf.org

National Italian American Sports Hall of Fame
   www.niashf.org

NYPD Columbia Association
   www.nypdcolumbia.org

Order Sons and Daughters of Italy
   www.osia.org

Primo Magazine
  www.flprimo.com/sellprimo.html

Pursuing Our Italian Names Together
  www.point-pointers.net

Recipes my Nonna taught me
  www.angelfire.com/oh2/cookbook/main.html

Skorupa's Italian-American Homepage
  www.members.aol.com/alskor/italo-amer.html

That's Italian
  homepage.interaccess.com/~chasd

The Florida Federation of Italian American Clubs
  ffiac.com

Tricolore
  www.tricolore.net

Umberto's Clam House
  www.umbertosclamhouse.com/?littleitalynyc

Uniting Single Italian Americans Worldwide
  community-2.webtv.net/mpinciotti/UnitingSingle/

United States Bocce Federation
  bocce.com

Wonderful world of Bocce
  www.sites2c.com/bocce

**If you enjoyed this book,
check out these iUniverse authors:**

Michael Crider
Dada
Dada: A Guy's Guide to Surviving Pregnancy, Childbirth, and the First Year of Fatherhood is the perfect gift for all new or expectant fathers and mothers alike. Author Michael Crider guides you through a laugh-filled tour of parenthood from a neurotic new father's point of view.

From the trials and tribulations of pregnancy to the end of the first year of fatherhood, **Dada** pulls no punches. Crider's wit and knack for pointing out the humor in even the most serious of situations makes **Dada** a must-read for all new parents.

Verne Edstrom, Esq.
Dr. Verne's Northern White Trash Etiquette
Need to brush up on your trailer park etiquette? If you feel like you're just not fitting into the lifestyle, look no further, everything you ever wanted to know from white trash career opportunities to cheating on your mate with success...it's all right here in this book!

Dr. Verne's Northern White Trash Etiquette isn't that wimpy self-help you'll get from creeps like Deepak Chopra and Stephen Covey. No, Dr. Verne dispenses practical, common sense advice for decent working people.

**Buy these books through your local bookstore
or at www.iuniverse.com.**

0-595-22168-8

Printed in the United States
1274400004B/289-291